The Story of
SUN TZU

www.royalcollins.com

Picture Story Book of
Ancient Chinese Thinkers

The Story of
SUN TZU

Xin Bingyong

Translated by Wu Meilian

Books Beyond Boundaries

ROYAL COLLINS

Picture Story Books of Ancient Chinese Thinkers
The Story of SUN TZU

Xin Bingyong
Translated by Wu Meilian

First published in 2024 by Royal Collins Publishing Group Inc.
Groupe Publication Royal Collins Inc.
BKM Royalcollins Publishers Private Limited

Headquarters: 550-555 boul. René-Lévesque O Montréal
(Québec) H2Z1B1 Canada
India office: 805 Hemkunt House, 8th Floor, Rajendra Place,
New Delhi 110 008

ISBN: 978-1-4878-1163-1

To find out more about our publications, please visit www.royalcollins.com.

He chose a simple life of farming and studying with big dreams in his heart when he was young.

He was brave and honest when training the army in Wu.

He used clever strategies in battles, winning against bigger armies with his smart thinking …

He loved peace but was not afraid of war.

The story of war and peace is like a rollercoaster, with ups and downs and finding a balance.

It is a part of the Chinese people's character and heritage.

Through exciting stories and colorful descriptions, you will discover the extraordinary life and amazing wisdom of a military hero.

Sun Wu, with the courtesy name Changqing, was also respectfully known as Sun Tzu (Master Sun). He was approximately a contemporary of Confucius, but his exact years of birth and death were uncertain.

A descendant of legendary emperor Shun and the seventh-generation offspring of Prince Wan of Chen, he is better remembered as "The Sage of War" from his military masterpiece *The Art of War* and the famous battle of Baiju.

The Lord of the State of Chen was surnamed Gui. They were the offspring of the legendary emperor Shun. When Prince Wan was born, his father, Duke Li, invited the Grand Historian of Zhou to divine the boy's fate. According to the prophecy, the boy would have a great future and carry forward the legacy of the Gui family. The prophecy was eventually fulfilled by his descendents in the State of Jiang.

When war broke out in the State of Chen, Duke Li was killed, and Prince Wan fled to the State of Qi. He refused the position of a high official offered by Duke Huan of Qi and became a court manager of craftsmen. He was thus also known as Tian Wan, after his fief in the region of Tian. Seeing that he was a highly capable person, the Qi aristocrat Yizhong married his daughter to Tian Wan. The divination result was very auspicious, showing that Wan's descendants would enjoy a prosperous future in Qi.

The Tian family did become influential during
the sixth generation after Tian Wan. Tian Shu, the
grandfather of Sun Wu, was a high official in Qi,
and he won an important war against the State of
Ju in 523 BCE. Because of his victory, Duke Jing of
Qi awarded him the surname of Sun and the fief of
Le'an. His son, Sun Ping, was even more elevated
than himself.

Born and raised in such a privileged family, Sun Wu
received a very good education and showed a strong
interest in military strategies.

When the Tian, Bao, Luan, and Gao families got into struggles for power, Sun Wu escaped to the State of Wu in eastern China. Usually, descendants of noble heritage could be officials in any state, but Sun Wu did not seek refuge under the Duke of Wu. He lived in seclusion in the mountains outside Gusu City (present-day Suzhou), where he farmed, studied, and wrote about lessons from important wars in the past.

In Gusu, Sun Wu met aristocrat Wu Yuan, courtesy name Zixu. Wu Yuan's father, Wu She, was the respected teacher of Chu Prince Jian. His assistant, Fei Wuji, was jealous of what Wu She received from the prince, so he framed him to have the King of Chu to banish the prince and killed Wu She and his oldest son, Wu Shang. Wu Zixu fled to the State of Wu and sought refuge under Duke Ji Guang.

In 515 BCE, Wu Zixu suggested Duke Ji Guang invite King Liao of Wu to dine at his home. During the party, Wu Zixu's sworn brother, Zhuan Zhu, offered a fish to the king and, before everyone understood, suddenly drew a small knife from the fish's belly and murdered the king.

Duke Ji Guang usurped the throne. He would later become the famous King Helü of Wu. He had a great ambition of dominating the world, and he hoped to achieve this goal with the help of Wu Zixu and another aristocrat Bo Pi who fled the State of Chu. However, he was worried that they were too obsessed with avenging their families and overlooking the interests of the State of Wu.

No one knew the king's struggle except Wu Zixu. He recommended Sun Wu to be the chief commander of the Wu army. King Helü was reluctant to assign such an important post to a nameless hermit, but Wu Zixu was determined and repeatedly persuaded the king to give Sun Wu a chance. The king finally agreed.

Sun Wu came to court. The king was satisfied with his heritage and shocked by his thirteen writings on military strategies. He was eager to find out the practical application of Sun Wu's theories.

"Can you design some games with your strategies?" the king asked.

"The art of war is a serious matter and not something to be played with," answered Sun Wu solemnly.

King Helü was very pleased by his answer. "Can you show me your strategies with the court maids?" he asked again.

Sun Wu understood the intention of the king, so he agreed but said, "Women are not used to wars, so they may look funny. I'm afraid my Lord would regret his decision." The king did not take this seriously and asked Sun Wu to carry out the test.

The next day, Sun Wu came to the imperial training ground. The place was surrounded by a big crowd. Everyone wanted to see this interesting event.

About 300 court maids were selected for the test, and their arrival provoked intense discussion among the audience.

Sun Wu divided the women into two groups and asked them to form teams according to height. He also appointed two of King Helü's royal wives team leaders.

Sun Wu stood at the front and showed the women directions and basic army knowledge.

"All your movements should follow the drum. Look forward if the drum directs you forward; look left and right when the drum directs you left and right; turn around if the drum directs you to go back. Do you understand?"

"Yes, sir," answered the maids.

Sun Wu brought them spears and demonstrated the rules again. By this time, the maids were very impatient, and they felt ridiculous when the test started. They laughed and joked and couldn't form teams at all.

King Helü watched and felt funny, too, but he wanted to see how Sun Wu dealt with the situation.

Sun Wu stopped the drum. He first harshly criticized himself as a commander and then emphasized the rules one more time. After that, he told the two group leaders to take up their responsibilities and lead their groups.

When the exercise began, the maids were still laughing and joking. Sun Wu was very angry; he summoned the law enforcement officer and asked, "What's the punishment for those who disobey the law in the army?"

"Beheading!" answered the officer.

Sun Wu immediately ordered the beheading of the two leaders. King Helü was shocked and asked Sun Wu to spare them. "I appreciate your ability to command an army. Please spare my two royal wives for my sake," said the king.

However, Sun Wu answered, "My Lord has given his words to perform this military exercise with these women, and you should not repent your decision. You should also know that a military commander's position is higher than that of the king in the army, so forgive me if I cannot listen to your order." With that said, Sun Wu gave an order to kill the two court ladies.

After this, he selected two other maids to be group leaders and continued the exercise. This time, the maids dared not be disrespectful, and their movement became very disciplined and professional. Sun Wu thus reported to the king, "My Lord, the army is trained. They will diligently carry out any orders you give them."

The king was still furious about what Sun Wu did to his royal wives. He answered coldly, "You may return now. I will not watch anymore."

Sun Wu smiled and said, "My Lord likes empty words in books more than practical application." He returned to his lodging and prepared to leave, but Wu Zixu persuaded him to stay.

The king, on the other hand, was still very upset about losing two wives. Wu Zixu met with him and said, "The art of war is no joke. If there is no punishment, then the rules will not be clear. No one else but Sun Wu can help my Lord conquer the Chu State and establish his name in the world."

King Helü realized his mistake and went to see Sun Wu.

Sun Wu apologized to the king but explained his reason for executing the two court ladies. He said, "The law of the army and the premise for winning is to award those who obey and punish those who don't." The king was fully convinced and officially appointed Sun Wu as a general.

Under Sun's rigorous training, the Wu army quickly became highly disciplined and invincible.

In 512 BCE, Wu Zixu and Sun Wu led the Wu army to attack the Chu State. They conquered the city of Shu and killed two brothers of the former king of Wu, who had fled to Chu. King Helü wanted to continue attacking the capital of Chu, but Sun Wu said, "The soldiers are exhausted. My Lord should wait."

Chu was a big and powerful state, and its King Zhao
of then was a wise and benevolent ruler who had just
killed the sinister officer Fei Wuji and was thus widely
supported by his people. King Helü was also aware it was
not the best time to fight Chu, so he adopted Sun Wu's
advice. After the war, Sun Wu continued to train the Wu
army and develop a plan of conquering the Chu.

Three years later, Duke Zhao of Cai went to see the
King of Chu and presented him with a luxurious
piece of jade and a fur coat. Zichang, a greedy official
in Chu, asked the Duke of Cai for the same gifts, but
the duke refused to give them. So, Zichang illegally
detained the duke in Chu for three years.

In the same year, Duke Cheng of Tang came to
see the King of Chu as well, and Zichang had his
eyes on the duke's beautiful horses. When the duke
refused his demand, Zichang detained him in Chu
for three years, too.

In the winter of 507 BCE, the followers of the two dukes finally persuaded their lords to present their treasures to Zichang so that they could be released to their countries. At this point, the States of Cai and Tang were extremely upset about Chu.

A year later, King Helü decided that his country was strong enough to fight Chu, so he summoned Wu Zixu and Sun Wu to discuss the plan.

Sun Wu said, "Chu is a big, powerful country. It is too risky to directly attack the capital Yingdu, so we must besiege with the help of Tang and Cai."

That autumn, the State of Cai defeated the State of Shen, a vassal of Chu. The Chu army immediately besieged Cai for revenge, and Cai sought help from Wu.

The time that Sun Wu had been waiting for finally arrived. King Helü, Wu Zixu, and Sun Wu joined the armies of Tang and Cai with 30,000 men. They quickly crossed the three passes of Dasui, Zhiyuan, and Ming'e in the north of Chu and arrived at the east bank of the Han River, face to face with the Chu army on the other side.

Seeing the enemy approaching, Zichang, the sinister Chu minister, decided to cross the river and fight with the Wu army. Sun Wu took advantage of his arrogance and quickly defeated him. This greatly hit the morale of the Chu army.

Zichang and the rest of the Chu army retreated to Baiju, near the capital. The Wu army was highly motivated, but Sun Wu warned them not to underestimate their enemy, since the Chu army had nothing to lose at this point, and they would fight as hard as they could.

The next morning, King Helü's brother Fugai decided to attack without Sun Wu's permission. He believed the Chu soldiers wouldn't fight for the sinister Zichang, so he led 5,000 men and advanced carelessly. Fortunately, this reckless action did not cause any serious outcome. The already desperate Chu army was soon completely defeated.

The Wu army pursued and destroyed the Chu army at Qingfashui and Yongshi. Zichang fled to the State of Zheng.

Without the protection of Baiju, the Chu capital could not resist the Wu army, which quickly occupied the city. This legendary victory of 30,000 troops over 200,000 won its place in the history of war in China, thanks to Sun Wu's military strategies.

Chu minister Shen Baoxu hurried to the State of
Qin and asked for help, but the King of Qin refused.
Shen Baoxu stood and cried outside the Qin court for
seven days and nights without eating or drinking. His
loyalty finally moved the king, who agreed to give him
500 war chariots to fight the Wu army.

King Helü of Wu was dazzled by the joy of victory and did not immediately return to his country as Sun Wu suggested. His brother Fugai secretly returned to Wu and usurped the throne. Helü finally took Sun Wu's advice and returned. He defeated Fugai, who fled back to Chu.

Two years later, King Helü ordered Sun Wu and Wu Zixu to help Prince Fuchai fight the State of Chu again. Hearing that Sun Wu was leading the troops, the frightened King of Chu moved the capital to Ruo to escape the attack.

Another three years passed. King Helü was injured in a battle against the State of Yue and soon passed away. Before he died, he asked Sun Wu to support his son, Fuchai, to carry on his career and fulfill his ambition.

His son and his ministers did not let him down. With Sun Wu and Wu Zixu's help, King Fuchai eventually defeated the State of Yue and became a powerful ruler of the State of Wu.

Apart from his remarkable military achievements, Sun Wu left future generations with a groundbreaking military masterpiece: *The Art of War*.

The Art of War consists of about 6,000 words in thirteen chapters. As the earliest military work in China, it has had a profound impact on the military of China as well as the world.

The Art of War teaches not only schemes and conspiracy in battles but also the wisdom of dealing with war. As he said, although war requires deceitful means, it requires more of a prudent attitude—to be neither arrogant nor impetuous, to both understand oneself and one's enemy—to win. The way of the king is to subdue without fighting.

The philosophical spirit of Sun Wu has long been integrated into the character of the Chinese nation, which values peace and has a fearless attitude toward power.

ABOUT THE AUTHOR

Xin Bingyong, born in 1954, graduated from the Art Department of East China Normal University. He is skilled in traditional Chinese painting, comic strips, and cartoons. He is a member of the China Artists Association and the Shanghai Artists Association and a standing director of the Shanghai Minmeng Calligraphy and Painting Academy. He is also the director of the Xin Bingyong Studio at the Shanghai Haipai Comic Strip Center. He has published more than 20 picture albums and comic strips.